No Limits

SNOWBOARDING

Jed Morgan

W

FRANKLIN WATTS
LONDON • SYDNEY

First published in 2005 by
Franklin Watts
96 Leonard Street
London
EC2A 4XD

Franklin Watts Australia
45–51 Huntley Street
Alexandria, NSW 2015

Series editor: Adrian Cole
Series design: Pewter Design Associates
Art director: Jonathan Hair
Picture researcher: Sophie Hartley

A CIP catalogue record for this book is available from the British Library.

ISBN: 0 7496 5824 X

Printed in Malaysia

The author and publisher would like to thank the following people
for their contribution to the production of this book: Burton Snowboards
(www.burton.com); K2 snowboards (www.k2snowboards.com); Nitro
Snowboards (www.nitrousa.com); all the staff at TSA©, the snowboard
asylum, Milton Keynes Xscape (www.snowboard-asylum.com)

Acknowledgements:
The Publisher acknowledges all © products shown within this
title as the property of their respective owners.
Brand X Pictures/Alamy: 20t. ImageState/Alamy: 8t, 20 b. StockShot/
Alamy: 17t, 23t. ©2003 John Birkett: 24t. © 2005 Burton Snowboards: 4,
5t & c, 10t & bl, 11tl & tr, 14bl. © 2005 Burton Snowboards (photo: Jeff
Curtes): 10br, 13br, 23br, 24b, 28t, 29l. © 2005 Burton Snowboards
(photo: Dean "Blotto" Gray): 13bl, 14t, 15t, 23bl, 25t, 26t. © 2005 Burton
Snowboards (photo: Vincent Skoglund): 25b. © 2005 Burton Snowboards
(photo: Kevin Zacher): 22. Adrian Cole: 9b. © Mike Chew/Corbis: 17b.
© Jeff Curtes/Corbis: 12, 13t. © Duomo/Corbis: 27t. © Picimpact/Corbis:
14br. © Reuters/Corbis: 9t, 19b, 26b. © Royalty-Free/Corbis: 21t.
© TempSport/Corbis: 5b. © Troy Wayrynen/NewSport/
Corbis: 18. Empics: 28b, 29t. Courtesy K2 (UK)
Limited: 6b, 6-7, 8b, 11cl, cr & b, 15b, 19t, 21b, 27b.
Board courtesy Nitro Snowboards (photo: Adrian
Cole): 7b. Tony Kyriacou/Rex Features: 16t. ©
Stockfile/Sang Tan: cover. Courtesy Xscape, Milton
Keynes: 16b.

Whilst every attempt has been made to clear copyright
should there be any inadvertent omission please apply
in the first instance to the publisher regarding rectification.

Impotant Note:

Disclaimer – In the preparation of this
book all due care has been exercised with
regard to the activities depicted. The
Publishers regret that they can accept no
liability for any loss or injury sustained.

Contents

World of snowboarding   4

Know your snowboard   6

A snowboard for all   8

Get geared up   10

Get ready to go   12

Play it safe   14

Just for fun   16

Snowboarding sports   18

Getting started   20

Moving on   22

Beyond the limits   24

Get serious!   26

Meet the pros   28

Jargon buster   30

Find out more   31

Index   32

World of snowboarding

Snowboarding is only 30 years old, but it is already one of the most popular and fastest growing winter sports. Whether meeting with friends to enjoy the great outdoors or taking part in serious competitions, snowboarding has it all.

Snowboarding is born

An American called Sherman Poppen is generally considered to be the inventor of the snowboard. In 1965 he joined two skis together to make a winter toy for his daughter. A rope was attached to the front to aid balance and the new toy was named the 'Snurfer' (from snow and surf). The word spread and soon Poppen was organising competitions and went on to sell over 500,000 Snurfer boards.

To the limit

Many people credit Tom Sims with the development of the very first snowboard in 1963. He was just thirteen years old when he made his 'ski board' in a design and technology lesson at school.

Snowboarders with the latest Burton boards back in the 1980s. It wasn't until then that snowboarding really took off.

Jake Burton

One of those people taking part in Poppen's competitions was Jake Burton. He went on to pioneer the modern snowboard. In 1977 Jake Burton developed the Snurfer by adding foot bindings to improve control and used laminated boards (see pages 6–7) for greater strength and flexibility. In 1980 he further developed his boards by adding a P-Tex (polyethylene) base to make them move faster across the snow. 'Burton' remains one of the leading snowboarding brands.

Jake Burton shaping a board tip. Burton Snowboards continue to develop snowboard technology today.

FROM THE EDGE

'Once people started riding snowboards in resorts and stuff, that opened up a whole new way for us to grow the sport. That's when I realised snowboarding was going to get a whole lot bigger.'
Jake Burton Carpenter

Winter Olympics

In 1998, snowboarding reached the ultimate goal when it became an official Olympic sport at the Nagano Winter Olympics in Japan. There were two snowboarding events in the Olympics for men and women: the Halfpipe and the Giant Slalom. The first Olympic Halfpipe competition was won by Gian Simmen (men) and Nicola Thost (women), while the Giant Slalom was won by Ross Rebagliati (men) and Karine Ruby (women). The Giant Slalom was replaced by the Parallel Giant Slalom at Salt Lake City in 2002 (see pages 18–19).

The Giant Slalom was one of the first snowboarding events to be included in the Winter Olympics.

Know your snowboard

Snowboards may look similar, but there are differences between the board styles (see pages 8–9). The K2 Instinct 153, shown here, is a good example of an all mountain freeride snowboard.

DECK (top layer above the core, shown here)
∗ Design — brightly decorated with cool designs, graphics and brand logos. The deck also has mounting holes for bolting the bindings firmly to the board.

Board laminate — Hybritech, patented K2 board laminate, including carbon, ceramic and Kevlar© layers

Board core (between the deck and base) — K2 bi-polar = strong, lightweight and designed to maximise speed

Binding mounting holes

TIP (front end, also called the nose)
∗ Design — rounded and turned upwards to help the board pass over the snow.

BINDINGS
These keep your boot firmly attached to the snowboard and allow you and the board to move as one. Bindings greatly improve the control you have over the board. There are various types of binding so it is best to seek expert advice when choosing them.

LEASH (not shown)
A strap that connects between your front leg and the front binding. It is a safety device that stops your board slipping away and becoming a hazard to other people. For this reason all ski and snowboard resorts insist on a leash.

TAIL (rear end)
✱ Design — usually rounded and flatter than the tip. A 'twin-tip' freestyle board allows the boarder to move in either direction with ease.

STOMP PAD (not shown)
A rubber or soft plastic mat stuck to the deck in between the bindings. A stomp pad is used when your back foot is out of the bindings such as when using a chairlift to get to the slope. Without a stomp pad your foot could slip off the board and cause you an injury.

Tail — Hybritech cap design, specially tapered to improve turns and for enhanced speed in powder snow

Base — 4000 Sintered, fastest natural ceramic base material available, very durable and retains wax longer

Edge — Rust resistant stainless steel, produces fewer burrs (see page 13) to increase control

BASE (below the core)
✱ Design — made of slick, hard-wearing material including P-Tex (polyethylene) or carbon.
✱ Wax — applied to the base to help it glide more easily across the snow.

Cool science

Snowboards are made of materials that are laminated. This is where several thin layers are sandwiched together using special glues. The different layers provide strength, flexibility and durability to the board whilst keeping it lightweight. Wood, foam, rubber, fibreglass, P-Tex and graphite are some of the materials that can be found in a modern snowboard.

EDGE
A narrow metal strip that runs along the side of the snowboard from the tip to the tail. The edge digs into the snow when the board is tilted to provide grip and help in turning. The 'toeside' is the edge nearest to your toes and the 'heelside' is that nearest to your heels.

A snowboard For all

It is important that you choose the right board for you. There are hundreds on the market, but before you rush out to spend your cash, first decide what type of board is right for your style of riding.

Freeriding / All mountain board

This is the most popular type of board and a good all-rounder. It will allow you to perform basic tricks, pick up good speed downhill and carve up a mountain circuit. Freeriding boards are of medium length and stiffness, making them good for a range of snow conditions. The tip and tail are also turned up which means they can be ridden backwards, or 'fakie', for a limited time, as well as forwards.

Freeriding boards are popular with boarders because of their versatility.

This is just one example of a growing number of freestyle boards on the market.

Freestyle / Technical board

These are shorter, fatter and more flexible than other boards and have a 'twin-tip' design. Their flexibility makes them ideally suited to the demanding spins and jumps associated with serious tricks and riding the halfpipe. The twin-tip makes them ideal for riding fakie. Freestyle boards also turn extremely well, which makes them a popular choice for first-timers.

Alpine / Carving board

Alpine boards are designed for maximum speed and fast turns, and are used for downhill and slalom racing. They are the longest, narrowest and stiffest of all snowboards. The length gives great stability while the stiffness helps the edges to carve into the snow. This allows the rider to perform high-speed turns — but not tricks.

Parallel giant slalom racing. Alpine boards are designed to allow the rider to travel as fast as possible.

HOT HINT

Once you've decided on the style of board you want, you'll need one that's your size. Check at your local snowboard shop, but you will need to consider the following:
* Your height – this affects the board length.
* Your weight – this affects the stiffness of the board you need to get.
* Your feet size – this affects the width of your snowboard.

Staff at your local snowboard shop can help you to choose the best board for you.

Junior boards

Snowboarding is especially popular with juniors and some begin boarding at only 3 years old! Some manufacturers now make junior versions of the different snowboards that are smaller and more flexible.

HOT HINT

If you're not sure which board you need, try hiring one first. Most board shops and winter resorts now have snowboard hire, and you can probably get all your gear there, too. Alternatively you could borrow a board from a friend.

Get geared up

Snowboarding gear isn't just about looking cool. It performs an important job keeping you safe, comfortable and warm. Of course if you look cool too, then that's a bonus!

Snowboard boots and bindings

Snowboard boots vary. The type you need will depend on the board and bindings you have. Soft boots allow greater movement and are normally used with freestyle or freeride boards. They fit into 'high-back' bindings or 'step-in' bindings. Alpine boards are normally used with hard boots. These have a soft inner boot, but a hard plastic outer shell to give you greater support in fast turns. Hard boots fit into flat 'plate' bindings.

A warm, waterproof jacket with a hood is essential. Remember, temperatures in mountain resorts will usually be around 0 degrees Celsius.

Clothing

What you wear for snowboarding will depend on the conditions you board in. The main thing is to make sure you are warm and dry. Experts suggest wearing layers of clothing so that you can adjust what you wear as conditions change. You will certainly need a durable and waterproof outer layer to protect you from the worst winter weather. Fleece clothing is an ideal middle layer to help keep you warm. Lightweight T-shirts and leggings made from synthetic materials (not cotton) are good for inner layers. Staff at your local snowboard shop will be able to help you choose the right sort of clothing.

Gloves

Strong waterproof gloves or mittens are vital for life on a snowboard. Make sure they have wrist gaiters to stop the snow getting in and look for ones with reinforced fingers and palms as these will last longer.

Eyewear

A good pair of sunglasses or goggles is essential to stop the glare from the snow and to protect your eyes from falling or blowing snow. Many are tinted to improve visibility in bright snow conditions.

Head to toe

If you can keep your head and feet warm then the rest of your body will also feel warmer. A good warm hat and socks will make sure the cold doesn't spoil your snowboarding adventures.

Before you get in the ski lift make sure that you have all your gear with you. Don't forget your day pack too (see page 14).

Body armour

Beautiful powder snow can hide rocks, branches and other obstacles. You should do everything you can to protect yourself against serious injuries. Get a high-quality helmet to help protect your head. Knee and elbow pads can be worn underneath your outer clothing. Wrist guards will reduce the chance of hand and wrist injuries after a heavy landing.

Get ready to go

Your body and board will work hard when you're snowboarding so getting them ready for action is important.

A good stretch

Stretching is a good way to get your muscles ready for action. A stretch should be a slow movement and not quick or jerky. When you feel your muscle go tense, stop stretching and hold that position for about 15 seconds. You should repeat each stretch several times and do the same stretches on both sides of your body. Here are some good stretches for snowboarding, but there are many more you could learn.

To the limit

'I've seen inexperienced boarders tear muscles as a result of not warming up. Most of the time they are off the snow for weeks.' Katsuko Inamoto, snowboard instructor

Quads

Sit down with both feet out in front of you. Lean to the left and bend your right leg back until you feel the front of your thigh (your quadriceps) begin to tighten. Do not overstretch. Repeat the stretch with your other leg. Stand up once you've completed both stretches several times and shake out your legs.

A quad stretch. Stretching can greatly reduce the chances of you damaging your muscles.

Groin

Sit with your feet apart. Lean forwards as far as you can, placing your hands on the floor. Stand up with your feet apart. Turn one foot to the side and bend your knee on that leg, leaning gently over as you do so. Keep your other leg out straight and the toes facing forwards. Lean gently on the bent knee to help keep your balance. Repeat on the other leg.

Starting a groin stretch. Only stretch as far as is comfortable. If you overstretch you might do more harm than good.

Waxing and deburring (right) are an essential part of board maintenance.

Board Fitness

Keeping your board in shape is best done by experts. Most shops and resorts will offer these facilities. The main jobs are keeping the base smooth and waxed and the metal edges clean and deburred. Get your board checked out at least once a year and always if you've had a big crash or think you may have damaged it.

Waxing

There are many different types of snowboard wax available. Which one you choose will depend on the snow conditions. Once the base is clean and dent-free, wax is melted onto it with a hot iron from tip to tail. This wax layer greatly improves the speed of your board.

Deburring

Rough edges will cause your board to drag on turns. Make sure they are regularly deburred using a hard stone. Ask someone experienced in board maintenance to show you how.

Play it safe

Snowboarding should be about fun and lots of it! But you also need to be careful and make sure you do not injure yourself or anyone else.

Extreme snowboarding like this is best left to the pros.

Take it slowly

It's all too easy to rush into attempting snowboard skills and tricks. But you won't learn them overnight. Even gaining basic competence takes time, practice and patience. Make sure you feel prepared before trying something new.

Stick to the path

Winter mountains are dangerous places with hazards such as hidden obstacles, avalanches and even wild animals! Resorts have clearly marked runs to make sure you are kept safe. These routes are normally ranked by how hard they are, using a colour system. So as well as keeping to the official runs, make sure you are on the right one for your ability.

Look out!

Always snowboard with someone else, so that one of you can get help in case of an injury. Good resorts can become busy places, too. Look out for other snowboarders and obstacles, and be prepared to stop or get out of the way quickly. Remember you will probably share the slope with people on skis and on foot.

HOT HINT

Get a waterproof day pack to carry your extras, such as sun cream and snacks. Carry a 'tune' kit too, including a spare leash (1), a hard stone (2), wax (3), stomp pads (4) and a multi-tool (5).

All runs are clearly marked.

Hanging on a platform in the sun. The sun can still damage your skin, even if you feel cold.

Watch the sun

It might be freezing cold and the middle of winter, but the sun can still do a lot of damage to your skin. This is especially true on snow, because it reflects UV (ultraviolet) light back up at you. To protect yourself use a high-factor sun cream (at least 30) on exposed skin and wear sun block on your lips. Take your sun cream with you so that you can re-apply it later in the day.

Energy levels

Snowboarding uses a lot of energy so you need to make sure you keep your body well fuelled. Carry some high-energy snacks such as dried fruit or chocolate and make sure you drink plenty of liquids.

HOT HINT

It's important to take breaks during your session to maintain your energy levels. Take the opportunity to grab a snack or top up your sun cream. Don't forget to stay warm though.

FROM THE EDGE

Know your Responsibility Code. Snowboard by it. Live by it.

✱ Always stay in control, and be able to stop or avoid other people or objects.

✱ People ahead of you have the right of way. It is your responsibility to avoid them.

✱ You must not stop where you obstruct a trail or are not visible from above.

✱ Whenever starting downhill or merging into a trail, look uphill and give way to others.

✱ Always use devices, such as a leash, to help prevent runaway equipment.

✱ Observe all posted signs and warnings. Keep off closed runs.

✱ Prior to using any ski lift, you must have the knowledge and ability to load, ride and unload safely.

Just For Fun

Snowboarding is a Winter Olympic sport with its own World Championships, but for most boarders it is simply a thrilling way to enjoy the great outdoors and have some fun.

Hoping for snow

If you are lucky enough to live in a mountainous area with lots of snow then you can probably enjoy snowboarding quite frequently. However, for millions of boarders it is either a case of setting off for the snow or hoping it comes to you. When it does come, even quite a gentle slope can give you the chance to call a friend and get on your boards, so make the most of it!

Snow on a hill in London. A snowboarder wastes no time in getting to grips with a recent snowfall — even though it barely covers the ground!

Checking out the slope at the snowdome, Milton Keynes.

Indoor snow

There are now many indoor snow slopes or 'domes' where you can ride on 'real' snow even in the mid-summer heat. They may not have the thrill of outdoors, but they allow you to try new skills and keep in practice. Some even have halfpipes (see pages 18–19) for trying out tricks.

To the limit

The snowdome at the Xscape centre in Milton Keynes, UK, is the largest in Europe. With two 170 m slopes and 'real' snow, it's a snowboarder magnet!

Snowboard holidays

Most people enjoy snowboarding as part of a winter holiday. Mountain resorts around the world welcome millions of snow-seekers every year and have everything you need. In fact, a holiday can be a good way to try out snowboarding for the first time. You can hire your board and boots, join in some lessons to learn the basics, and then try out different styles and routes, or even the halfpipe.

When you become more experienced you could even try out extreme snowboarding holidays such as heli-snowboarding. This is where you are taken in a helicopter to really remote (and steep) mountains with some of the best snow and scenery in the world. The helicopter drops you at the top and collects you at the bottom.

To the limit

On 20 April 1998 Tammy McMinn (USA) snowboarded down a slope in British Columbia, Canada, 101 times. A helicopter took her to the top each time. She snowboarded a total distance of 93,123 m (305,535 ft) — a world record!

FROM THE EDGE

'The whole snowboarding experience was so overwhelmingly awesome that I couldn't fully appreciate it until I returned home and had time to rewind the images in my memory. So much beauty that it was a sensory overload!' Kathy Berman, following her heli-snowboarding holiday

Season pass

If you live within easy reach of guaranteed snow then it might be worth you buying a season pass. These work in many ways, but in general will allow you access to the slopes as often as you like during the season. They usually include a lift pass, too. Over time, a pass will save you lots of money.

A season pass will give you access to the slopes whenever they're open.

Snowboarding sports

If simply having fun is not enough for you then how about getting into snowboarding as a sport? There are several events to choose from, with professional competitors as young as just 13 or 14.

Slalom

The ultimate test in alpine snowboarding is the slalom. Competitors must get down the mountain by passing in between gates positioned along the course. There are several different events ranging from the Slalom to the Super G. The Slalom is over a short course with many gates and is quite slow. The Super G is over a much longer course with fewer gates and riders can reach speeds of over 100 kph!

All Slalom races are against the clock, with the fastest rider winning. An interesting twist on this is the Parallel Slalom and Parallel Giant Slalom. In these races riders go head to head down parallel courses. The loser is knocked out in each round until there is an eventual winner. Parallel Giant Slalom is an exciting spectator sport and the only Olympic Slalom event.

FROM THE EDGE

'Good racers begin their slalom race before they ever enter the starting gate. They scout out the fastest lines, and inspect every turn. They memorise every pole, bump and rut, then visualise their race to prepare themselves mentally.'
Scott Downey, snowboard coach and former pro snowboarder

Manuela Riegler of Austria makes a turn in a parallel slalom race. These have to be timed to perfection in order to record the fastest time.

Halfpipe

If tricks and big air are your thing then the halfpipe is your sport. Competitors ride along the halfpipe course in a zigzag fashion using their speed to launch off the rim of the halfpipe and perform mid-air tricks and turns. These are scored by a panel of judges according to their difficulty and how well they were performed. The thrills of the halfpipe mean it is one of the most popular events of the Winter Olympics.

Brian Savard performs a Mute grab on the lip of a halfpipe.

To the limit

The final of the men's halfpipe competition was watched by over 30,000 spectators at the 2002 Winter Olympics in Salt Lake City, USA.

Snowboard Cross or Boardercross

This is one of the most exciting of all snowboarding events. Six riders go head to head down a course that combines a mixture of turns, kickers, bumps and jumps. There is great excitement as they use all of their skills and strength to try and get ahead and then stay ahead! Races are in heats with the top three qualifying for the next round. It is not an Olympic sport yet, but there are hopes that it may be in the future.

FROM THE EDGE

'The key to winning is being the first one out of the gates. It can be tough because you never know what the other riders are gonna do. They could accidentally clip you and then your race is over, so you have to be careful how aggressively you race and when you decide to pass.' Drew Nielson, Boardercross competitor

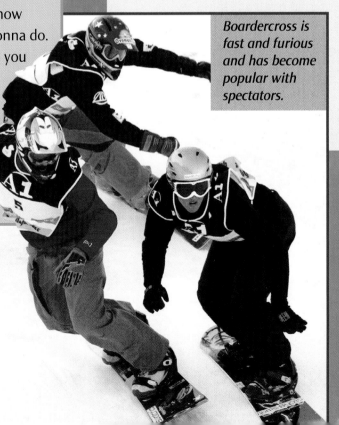

Boardercross is fast and furious and has become popular with spectators.

Getting started

It is tempting to hit the snow as soon as you have your board and gear, but it is worth taking your time to master the basics first.

Get on board

The first thing you must master is getting into your bindings. The best way to do this is to sit down and dig the heelside of your board into the snow to stop it slipping. Get into your bindings and make sure they are firmly fastened. Remember to put the safety leash on first.

To stand, pull your feet in close to your body and grab the toeside of your board with your back hand. Rock gently forwards, pull with your arm and straighten your legs to stand. You may find it easier to roll over so that your toeside is in the snow. You can then use both arms to push yourself up into a standing position.

Regular or goofy?

Snowboarders stand sideways with one foot in front of the other. If you stand with your left foot in front then you are a regular rider, but if your right foot is in front then you're a goofy. You normally stand with your strongest foot at the back of the board. So, if you are right footed (which do you kick a ball with?), then you will most likely be a regular boarder.

Stance

This is the distance between your feet on the snowboard. You can vary your stance by fixing your bindings into different holes on the snowboard. A good starting point is to set your bindings about shoulder width apart. Try different settings until you feel comfortable — a good stance is vital for snowboarding.

HOT TIP

The key to success is to stay relaxed. Keep your knees slightly bent and loosen your shoulders – this should help you to feel more comfortable and in control.

Finding your balance

Snowboarding is all about good balance. Start off with just your front foot in the bindings and slide slowly across a flat surface, pushing with your back foot. Next try sliding with your back foot loose but on the stomp pad (see page 7). When you feel ready, get into your bindings and get used to the feel of your snowboard by rocking gently between the toe and heel sides. You can also try crouching and standing again whilst slowly sliding. Use your arms to help you balance.

FROM THE EDGE

'The key to getting the most from snowboarding is expert instruction. By learning correctly the first time, your day becomes that much better. With every successful turn and stop you will build confidence and relish the sense of accomplishment.' Find My Adventure website (www.findmyadventure.com)

Moving on

Once you have mastered the basic skills it is time to move on to some more-advanced skills and tricks. The only way to learn how to do these properly is from a qualified snowboard instructor.

Skidded turns

These are the basic turns you will need to get boarding. Choose a gentle slope to begin with and set off slowly. To do a toeside turn look where you want to go. Slowly shift more weight over your front foot and tilt onto the balls of your feet. The board will begin to turn. As it does, bend your knees a little more and lean slightly into the turn. If you keep turning you will come to a stop.

HOT HINT

Many of the most impressive snowboarding tricks take hundreds of hours to master. You could cause yourself or other people serious injury if you try to do them before you're ready — so don't rush in.

Stopping

To make a stop, do a skidded turn, but as you come to right angle across the fall line (the natural line of descent) lean hard on the upper edge of your board and balance your weight equally over both feet. This will bring you to a controlled stop. Leaning into the slope with your knees bent can help, but remember to straighten as you slow, otherwise you will fall over.

Ollie

This is a move borrowed from skateboarding. It is a simple jump that can help clear an obstacle or give you extra height off a kicker or ramp. To do an Ollie, lean back to transfer your weight onto the tail of the board. Pull up with your front foot and then push down with your back foot to make the board spring off the ground. As you take off, pull your knees up into your body to gain extra lift. Try and keep your board level in mid-flight and as you prepare to land. Keep your weight in the middle of the board and bend your knees as you touch down. They will act like shock absorbers to cushion the impact of your landing.

'I fell over so many times when I was learning to snowboard, but don't give up, you'll soon get the hang of it. Everyone falls over, no matter what they might tell you!'
Laura Summers, snowboarding instructor

A Method Air — once perfected it looks this good!

Frontside 360 with a Mute. Adding a full rotation of 360 degrees gives you bonus points.

Grabs

Once you are confident with your ollie, try some mid-air grabs, such as a Mute Air, Indy Air or Method Air to add a bit of style to your routine. To perform a Method Air, grab the heelside edge of your snowboard between the bindings with your front hand, pull the board up behind you as high as your head. You need big air for this one!

Beyond the limits

New board technology and a new generation of young snowboarders mean the limits of snowboarding are being pushed. Who will be the new stars of the sport in the coming years and what tricks will they be pulling?

Mason Aguirre

Born in 1987, Mason follows his sister Molly in making a big impact as one of snowboarding's hottest new stars. 2004 was Mason's breakthrough year with major results including fourth in the US Open Halfpipe, second in the New Zealand Open Halfpipe, and seventh in the X-Games Halfpipe — the ultimate competition. He is well known for pushing the limits and includes incredible tricks in his pipe routines. These include the almost impossible 1080 (three full rotations in the air) that only a few people in the world can do.

Mason in the halfpipe at the US Snowboarding Grand Prix, Breckenridge, Colorado.

To the limit

Molly Aguirre is a star in her own right – riding the halfpipe and superpipe. She finished tenth in the 2004 X-Games Superpipe event.

Family ambitions

The Teter family are an incredible success story in the snowboarding world. The two brothers, Abe and Elijah, and their younger sister Hannah have all had top competition finishes and all are in the US snowboarding team. Hannah, at just 17 years old, enjoyed particular success in 2004. Some of her wins included the X-Games Halfpipe, two World Cup events and the Vans Triple Crown. She says her key to success is pushing women's snowboarding that bit further. She also pulls giant tricks that are normally only seen in the men's competition. She is one of the few women to regularly pull a frontside 900 (two and a half rotations in the air) in competition events. Hannah's big ambition, like her brothers, is to compete in the next Winter Olympics.

Hannah grabs huge air during a photo shoot. For many amateur snowboarders, including men, she is a constant source of inspiration.

FROM THE EDGE

'Since the guys have been the 'bringer uppers' of this sport, they kind of run the show. I mean girls rock, don't get me wrong, but the guys for some reason always bust out just huge airs and awesome tricks, some of which women have never attempted. They have no advantages; they're just men, who have been the dominant figures for a very long time.' Hannah Teter

Get serious!

Most people will only get a chance to enjoy snowboarding every now and again, but if you are really serious then here are a few tips to take it further.

Practice makes perfect

Good snowboarders practise for hours on end. They experiment and see just how far they can push themselves and their board. You may not be able to get onto the snow, but find out if there is an indoor snowdome in your area. These can be great for practising moves and exercising. Then you'll be in shape for when you hit the slopes. You can even practise your weight balance and tilting at home, but make sure you have a clear area first.

Snowboarders will practise tricks against almost anything.

Kelly Clark of the USA on her Winter Olympics, gold medal-winning halfpipe run. Thousands of people came to watch the games in Salt Lake.

Learn from others

Your local snowboard shop or centre should have information about any events that are coming your way. Go and see as many of these as you can afford. They are a great way to learn from the experts and pick up useful tips. As you get better there may even be events that you could enter and get noticed by the pros! If you live near a resort or an indoor centre find out if there are snowboarding clubs you can join.

(Left to right) Doriane Vidal (silver), Kelly Clark (gold) and Fabienne Reuteler (bronze) on the medal podium in 2002.

Go for gold!

The ultimate prize in snowboarding is an Olympic gold medal, but these only take place every four years. The other main competition is the Snowboarding World Championship that takes place every other year. The next ones are in Switzerland in 2007 and South Korea in 2009. The key annual competition is the World Cup series. This involves around 20 meetings during the winter season (September–March) that take place in countries around the world from Chile to Japan. The World Cup series and World Championships include events such as Snowboard Cross that are not part of the Olympics. They also include the Big Air competition where riders launch from a jump and perform tricks such as the 720 Air (two complete mid-air spins).

Hard work...but worth it

To be a pro snowboarder is hard work. You have to keep physically fit and there is a lot of travelling involved. It is also very expensive, but most top riders are sponsored by manufacturers to help them with this. Some also earn money from making snowboarding videos that show off the real extremes of the sport. They are well worth watching for some amazing boarding action.

HOT TIP

Get to know the staff at your local snowboard shop. They are a great source of information about local clubs, lessons and events.

To the limit

Shaun White of the USA began competing as a professional snowboarder in 1999 when he was just 13 years old – the youngest pro ever!

Shooting a snowboarding film. These films demand the best and craziest tricks, such as this high wall rail.

Meet the pros

As snowboarding has become more popular, so have the big names. However, with newcomers constantly arriving on the slopes there are some exciting new faces, too.

Legends of snowboarding

People like Jake Burton and Tom Sims, who helped to pioneer the development of the modern snowboard, have become snowboarding legends. Their companies are still involved in cutting-edge design today and also sponsor many of the most exciting new riders.

Jake Burton has retired from professional snowboarding, but continues to influence the sport today.

To the limit

Rider profile:

In terms of pure winning success, Karine Ruby from France is the most successful snowboarder ever. She was the first woman to win an Olympic snowboarding title at the 1998 Winter Olympics in Nagano, Japan, and followed this with silver at the 2002 games. Between 1996 and 2003 she also claimed 6 World Championship gold medals and 3 silver medals. In the World Cup she has had 121 podium finishes including 68 wins! She started boarding in 1988 at just 10 years old and was still active in the 2004 season as the top-ranking woman in Boardercross.

Airborne heroes

The Halfpipe and Big Air events certainly pull in the crowds and can turn competitors into true heroes. The world's top two halfpipe riders in 2004 were Risto Mattila of Finland for the men and Soko Yamaoka of Japan for the women. Simon Ax of Sweden was the best big air performer in 2004. He was also the silver medallist at the World Championships in 2003 (behind Risto Mattila). There is no Big Air competition for women at the moment.

To the limit
Rider profile:

Soko Yamaoka of Japan won her first Halfpipe World Cup event at Laax, Switzerland, in 2002. Since then she has consistently finished on the winners' podium.

To the limit
Rider profile:

Ross Powers of the USA is the only person to have won two Olympic medals in the Halfpipe competition, with a bronze in 1998 and a gold in 2002. He's one of the most successful male boarders ever. In 2005 he finished first in the men's Halfpipe event in the FIS North American Cup held at Mount Bachelor.

Jargon buster

air — a trick which requires height from a jump. Also refers to the height achieved, for example a high jump achieves 'big air'.

Boardercross — also called snowboard cross, an event in which riders race against each other in groups of four to six.

carbon (fibre) — a material added to snowboards to improve flexibility.

carving — cutting a deep line in the snow on a turn.

Fakie — when a snowboarder rides in the opposite stance, for example a regular rider rides goofy.

Frontside — 1) a type of air in which you jump clockwise. 2) The toeside of the snowboard.

Giant Slalom — similar to the slalom, but the race winner is the person who rides quickest over two different courses. There is also a Parallel Giant Slalom event.

halfpipe — a 'U'-shaped course carved out of compacted snow. The walls vary between 1.5–3 metres in height. Also the name given to the event involving the course.

kicker — a specially shaped mound of snow designed to give riders good air.

laminate — when several different materials are stuck together to form a sheet. Snowboards are made from different types of laminate.

leash — a strap that connects the rider to his or her snowboard and prevents it from sliding away after a crash.

powder — pure, white fluffy snow.

P-Tex (polyethylene) — a type of hard-wearing plastic used on the base of snowboards.

rail — to move along a rail, wall or similar surface. There are different ways to rail.

Slalom — a snowboarding event that involves a long course with multiple gates, which must be passed correctly. The fastest time wins.

stomp pad — a pad stuck between bindings to stop the rider's foot slipping.

Super G — a fast event run on a downhill course which comprises jumps and turns. The fastest time wins.

Superpipe — a longer and wider course based on the halfpipe design.

synthetic — a material produced artificially, such as polyester – not naturally, like cotton.

wax — a solid substance that is melted onto the base of a snowboard to improve the speed at which it travels.

Find out more

Every effort has been made by the Publishers to ensure that these websites contain no inappropriate or offensive material. However, because of the nature of the Internet, it is impossible to guarantee that the contents of these sites will not be altered. We strongly advise that Internet access is supervised by a responsible adult.

www.fis-ski.com

The official website of the International Ski Federation that oversees the major international snowboarding competitions. Site includes all the latest competition results.

www.abc-of-snowboarding.com

A fantastic site with loads of information about everything related to snowboarding. Includes animations of basic tricks to help you learn.

www.snowboarding.com

This informative site has loads of news about the latest trends, new gear and the main competitions. Also features information on where to go snowboarding and a 'how to' section to improve your technique.

www.transworldsnowboarding.com

News, tips, products, holidays and anything else you want to know about snowboarding can be found here. There are some great photos of real extreme action!

www.snowboardaustralia.org.au

Informative site filled with competition reports, industry news, pictures and even a trading post where you can buy and sell snowboard gear.

www.expn.com

This site includes coverage of the Winter X-Games, with photos, rider profiles and all the latest news and results from one of snowboarding's ultimate events.

www.thebsa.org

The British Snowboarding Association website includes links to UK resorts and recommended instructors.

www.boarderzone.com

New Zealand snowboarding site that thinks local but rides global! Features a picture gallery and message board.

Index

Aguirre, Mason 24
Aguirre, Molly 24
alpine board 9, 10

balance 21
big air 19, 23, 30
Big Air event 27, 29
bindings 5, 6, 7, 10, 20, 21
board
  base 6, 7
  core 6
  deck 6, 7
  edge 7
  tail 7, 8, 13
  tip 5, 6, 7, 8, 13
Boardercross 19, 28, 30
board maintenance 13
Burton, Jake 5, 28
Burton snowboards 4, 5

carving 8, 9, 30
carving board see entry for
  alpine board
clubs 26

day pack 11, 14

fakie 8, 30
falling over 23
freeride board 6, 8, 10
freestyle board 7, 8, 10

Giant Slalom 5, 30
grabs 19, 23

halfpipe 8, 17, 19, 26, 30

Halfpipe event 5, 19, 24, 25,
  29, 30
heelside 7, 20
hiring gear 9
history 4–5
holidays 17

junior boards 9

K2 Instinct 153 6
kicker 19, 23, 30

laminate 5, 6, 7, 30
leash 7, 14, 15, 20, 30

McMinn, Tammy 17
mountain board see entry for
  freeride board

Parallel Giant Slalom 5, 9,
  18, 30
Parallel Slalom 18
Poppen, Sherman 4, 5
Powers, Ross 29

rail 27, 30
Responsibility Code 15
riding style also see entry
  for fakie 8
Ruby, Karine 5, 28

safety 14–15
Sims, Tom 4, 28
skidded turns 22
skills 20–21, 22–23
Slalom event 9, 18, 30

snowboard Cross see entry
  for Boardercross
snowboard gear 10–11
snowboard instructor 22
snowboard shop 9, 26
snowdome 16, 26
sponsorship 27
stance 20, 21, 30
starting out 20–21
stomp pad 7, 14, 21, 30
stopping 22
stretching exercises 12, 13
Super G event 18, 30
superpipe 24, 30

technical board see entry for
  freestyle board
Teter, Hannah 25
toeside 7, 20, 22, 30
tricks 8, 9, 14, 19, 22, 23, 24,
  25, 26, 27
tune kit 14
turning 7, 8 also see entry for
  skidded turns

wax or waxing 7, 13, 14, 30
White, Shaun 27
Winter Olympics 5, 16, 18,
  19, 25, 26, 27, 28
Winter X-Games 24, 25
World Championship 16, 27,
  28, 29
World Cup series 27, 28

Yamaoka, Soko 29